Be an eco hero

Outdoors

Sue Barraclough

W

FRANKLIN WATTS

LONDON•SYDNEY

First published in 2010
by Franklin Watts

Copyright © Franklin Watts 2010

Franklin Watts
338 Euston Road
London NW1 3BH

Franklin Watts Australia
Level 17/207 Kent Street
Sydney, NSW 2000

All rights reserved.

Series editor: Sarah Peutrill
Art director: Jonathan Hair
Design: Big Blu Design
Illustrator: Gary Swift

Dewey number: 363.7
ISBN 978 0 7496 9339 8

Printed in China

Franklin Watts is a division of
Hachette Children's Books,
an Hachette UK company.
www.hachette.co.uk

Picture credits:
Douglas Adams/Shutterstock:
12. Angelafoto/istockphoto: 11. Awilli/
Corbis: front cover. Steve Baines/
istockphoto: 6. Judy Barranco/
istockphoto: 10. Andi Bergar/
Shutterstock: 8b. bncc369/istockphoto:
9. Pattie Calfrey/istockphoto: 26.
Tony Campbell/istockphoto: 13t.
Phillip Danze/istockphoto: 19t.
Sharon Dominick/istockphoto: 15br.
Kristen Eckstein/istockphoto: 13b.
Jeff Greenberg/Alamy: 22. Hallgerd/
Shutterstock: 16. René Jansa/
istockphoto: 15tl. Rene Lee/istockphoto:
8t. Maxstockphoto/Shutterstock: 23b.
Roger McClean/istockphoto: 25t.
Tim Pannell/Corbis: 21. Piero Pazzi/
istockphoto: 20. Thomas Perkins/
istockphoto: 15tr. pdtnc/istockphoto:
23t. Photocreate/Shutterstock: 25b.
Ralph125/istockphoto: 23c. Recycle
Now Partners: 17tl, 17tr, 17bl, 17bl.
Audrey Roorda/istockphoto: 15cr.
Eva Serrabassa/istockphoto: 15bl.
Shutterlist/Shutterstock: 18. Erich
Spieldiener/istockphoto: 15cl. Sygma/
Corbis: 27b. Tramper/Shutterstock:
24. Jason van der Valk/istockphoto: 7.
Wishlist Images: 27t. Paul Woodson/
istockphoto: 14. Every attempt has
been made to clear copyright. Should
there be any inadvertent omission
please apply to the publisher for
rectification.

Contents

Find out ways to help your planet in this book and become an eco hero like me!

Words in **bold** are in the glossary on page 28.

Outdoor places

Our homes are in cities, towns and villages. All these places are also homes and **habitats** to other animals and plants.

You can be an eco hero by learning about your **environment.** There is a lot you can do to keep your environment clean and **healthy.** Looking after habitats helps the animals and plants that live in them.

Eco heroes look after the environment!

Our planet

Our environment is the planet we live on. It has the things we need to live, such as:

- air to breathe
- water to drink
- soil to grow food.

Our environment also gives us medicines, **fuels** and **materials** to make things.

The problem is that many of the things we all do **pollute** and damage the environment. Pollution makes the air, soil and water dirty and unhealthy. Using less and making less rubbish cuts down pollution. This is better for plant and animal habitats.

Living things

You can be an eco hero by learning about living things. Your environment is made up of an amazing mixture of different plant and animal life.

An eco hero knows:

- You can learn a lot by watching wildlife.
- If you pick a leaf or flower, or break a branch, you can harm an animal's habitat or food.
- If you do pick things up you should put them back where you found them.

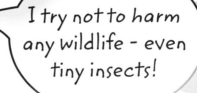

I try not to harm any wildlife - even tiny insects!

Web of life

Eco heroes know that all animals and plants are part of a **web** of life. All the animals and plants need each other to live and grow.

Insects are small animals that play an important part in the web of life. Bees and butterflies help plants make their **seeds** by carrying **pollen** from flower to flower.

Seeds can grow into new plants. Some plants need birds to eat and spread their seeds.

Earthworms eat dead leaves and help to break them down so plants can use the **nutrients** to grow.

Plants for life

Trees are the biggest plants. Trees are an important part of the web of life. Animals need trees for food and shelter.

If there were no plants, there would be no air to breathe or food to eat. Trees and other plants make **oxygen**, which humans and other animals need to breathe.

Plants give us:

Food to eat

Eco heroes know we need to look after plants.

Fuel

Material to make things **Oxygen to breathe**

And much more!

Growing plants

You can be an eco hero by growing plants for flowers and food. Grow plants in pots or window boxes if you don't have a garden. Make sure your plants have plenty of water and sunlight.

Before you **recycle** or throw away things, see if you can use them for gardening. Old CDs scare away birds that might eat your seeds. Cut the bottom off a plastic bottle to make a **cloche** for a **seedling**.

CD bird-scarer

Plastic bottle cloche

Lollystick label

Yogurt plant pot

There are lots of ways to reuse things in the garden. See if you can find different ways.

Recycling nature

If you have a garden or yard, you can be an eco hero by making **compost** from kitchen and garden waste. Compost is full of nutrients that plants need to grow.

Don't throw out your apple cores – put them in the compost!

18

Inside your compost bin, earthworms and other creatures, such as slugs and beetles, eat the waste. They help it to **rot** and break it down.

Earthworms also keep the rotting material healthy by making holes that let air in and water out.

Finally, in about a year, the waste is broken down into compost. You can add compost to soil to help plants grow.

Compost

Helping wildlife

You can be an eco hero by doing simple things to help wildlife. For example, keeping your cat indoors at night (especially at sunrise and sunset) stops them killing so many mice and birds.

Bell

A noisy bell on a cat's collar keeps birds and other small animals safe.

Be an eco hero by:

- Putting out food and water for birds regularly. If you feed birds, they have more babies. So if you stop putting out food, there may not be enough food for all the birds.
- Making sure you put out the right food for wildlife. Feeding wildlife the wrong food can be very bad for them (see page 29).

If you put out food for the birds, make sure feeders are high up so cats cannot reach them.

Take litter home

Take litter home with you to reuse or recycle, or put it in a bin. Make sure you only leave footprints when you go home.

Try to leave places as you found them.

- Litter such as metal cans takes many years to break down.
- If you throw something in a rubbish bin, it will go to a **landfill site** and we are running out of room to bury rubbish.
- Litter is dangerous for wildlife.

Nature spotter

We need to learn more about plant and animal habitats. Many animals and plants are dying out because habitats have been destroyed by farming and other human activities.

I found out that newts are in danger because their habitats are disappearing!

NEWTS

Be an eco hero by:

- Making a note of birds and other animals you have seen where you live.
- Sending your information to nature groups who can use it to help wildlife.
- Looking out for information about surveys on TV and on the Internet.

Watch the birds

Make a record

eco hero activities

Here are some more simple ways you can get active to be an eco hero outdoors.

If you have the space, plant your own tree. Choose a tree that you know is popular with wildlife. Or you can choose a tree for its fruit. Remember to find out how big a tree will grow before you make your choice.

Collect pet hair, dead grass, scraps of cotton and pieces of wool. Stuff it in an old fruit net. Hang it high in a tree in the spring and watch the birds collect materials to build their nests.

This family is helping to clean a beach.

Find out about wildlife organisations close to where you live. You and your family can help local groups by joining in with clean-up operations at wildlife areas such as ponds and beaches.

Glossary

cloche   a glass or plastic cover to keep tiny plants safe and warm.

compost   a soft, brown substance made from rotted plant material. You can make compost in a special bin.

environment   the space around you. It can be a building, a garden, a playground or a busy street. It can even include the whole planet.

fuel   the material used to make heat or light, usually by being burned. Coal, gas and oil are types of fuel.

habitat   a home for a plant or animal.

healthy   to be fit and well.

landfill site   a huge hole in the ground where rubbish is buried.

material   a substance that is used to make things.

nutrient   a substance that plants get from soil that they need to live and grow.

oxygen   a type of gas that animals need to live. A gas is an air-like substance that you cannot see.

pollen   a powder made by flowers.

pollute   to make air or water dirty.

recycle   to use materials again to make them into something new.

rot   to go slimy or mouldy and break down.

seed   the part of a plant from which a new plant can grow.

seedling   a tiny plant that grows from a seed.

web   a net-like structure made of thin threads. If one thread breaks the web falls apart.

Learn more

This book shows you some of the ways you can be an eco hero. But there is plenty more you can do outdoors to save the planet. Here are some websites that can help you learn more:

www.rspb.org.uk/youth
Lots of information about getting involved in campaigns and competitions, plus great games and activities.

www.actionfornature.org/action.html
Eco awards, nature friendly information and fun and games.

www.kidsplanet.org/wol/index.html
Find out more about the amazing web of life.

www.wildlifewatch.org.uk
Discover your local wildlife trust and the activities they run.

www.rspca.org.uk
You can find information about feeding wildlife on this site. Follow links to: Animal care and then click on: Wildlife advice.

www.naturedetectives.org.uk
Learn all about wildlife – from collecting and planting tree seeds to hunting for minibeasts. Also plenty of quizzes and games.

www.bbc.co.uk/nature/animals/birds/thingstodo/
Find out how to help birds.

Note to parents and teachers: Every effort has been made by the Publishers to ensure that these websites are suitable for children, that they are of the highest educational value, and that they contain no inappropriate or offensive material. However, because of the nature of the Internet, it is impossible to guarantee that the contents of these sites will not be altered. We strongly advise that Internet access is supervised by a responsible adult.

Index